Sun Come Back

Sun Come Back

—————— Poems ——————

BY

Daniel Newcomer

RESOURCE *Publications* · Eugene, Oregon

SUN COME BACK
Poems

Resource Publications
An Imprint of Wipf and Stock Publishers
199 W. 8th Ave., Suite 3
Eugene, OR 97401

www.wipfandstock.com

PAPERBACK ISBN: 978-1-5326-0338-9
HARDCOVER ISBN: 978-1-5326-0340-2
EBOOK ISBN: 978-1-5326-0339-6

VERSION NUMBER 01/02/26

All the things we love become memories one day.

This book is dedicated to my wife, Thea, and the memories we continue to make. It is also dedicated to our dog, Wiki, and the adventures we shared during his short time on earth, which will live in our hearts forever.

Contents

Acknowledgments

"Sun Come Back" was originally published in the *Dreams and Nightmares* poetry journal, Issue 122. September 2022.

"I haven't been around enough to judge the people in this town" was originally published in Issue #7 of *The Journal of Undiscovered Poets*. Copyright 2025. 7moredays Publishing.

Prologue

It began when a witch visited me in the barn where I was living, in the bucolic countryside deep in Germany's Black Forest, a few dozen kilometers outside the town of Freiburg im Breisgau. It was a cold and black night in the middle of December, and I kept warm in that barn by sleeping under a pile of hay the size of a horse carriage. The witch woke me by placing one hand on my chest and the other over my mouth, silencing the screams that rose inside me. Her eyes were all white, her face like a raisin, and when she spoke, her voice was quiet but scraped like fingernails breaking on a blackboard.

I will never forget her voice.

"You are cursed to wander with loneliness for the rest of eternity," she said.

When my desire to scream abated, she moved her hand that smelled of sweet milk from my mouth to my throat.

"I have already been cursed, ma'am. Don't you see?" I managed to say. "I've lost everything. My life, my home. Now I live in this barn. I *am* alone."

"I disagree, for being alone is no curse," she said. Her laugh was a cackle. "Loneliness is not the absence of people. It is when you find you cannot communicate and share whatever you believe is important. From here on out, you are destined to be at peace when in motion, forever to wander in joy. But your terror will be isolation only when you're with people, wherever you go. A solitude you can't understand. The smell of a leper you can't shake."

She removed her milk-scented hand from my throat and retreated into the shadows. Her pure white eyes disappeared in a blink.

Upon waking the next morning, I gathered my few possessions and left the barn, knowing full well the extra weight in my rucksack was from the terrible words she spoke.

And the witch was right. Since that fateful night of my cursing, I've spent my years wandering happily but always alone. I have seen perhaps a million people on six continents, but I have never made a single friend. Never found a dearest lover. I moved like a ghost through vast empty prairies and colorful mountain valleys where the only sound was the whisper of fog. I was a detached spectator in cities that moved like anthills and in towns steeped in fundamentalist fervor, traversing borders and cultures, and when I begged, no one had a dollar to give. I lived everywhere from the demon-scoured, ancient forests to the frigid rivers, lakes, seas, and oceans, where hands from Hell reached up through the water's soup-like floor to tickle the bottom of my feet, as if I were no more than their plaything.

In the Americas. In Europe. Asia. Africa and Australia. I have done nothing but wander from place to place, always alone, no matter how hard I've tried to connect.

I confronted beauty that took my breath away, my lungs shriveling to make space for a heart that grew four times its size to the point of exploding, but there was no one to share the moment with me and say, "Isn't this the most wonderful thing on Earth you have ever seen?"

I confronted the ugly, too.

I saw how suffering was like love. People, animals, nature: their love and pain existed in perfect harmony. And when I was suffering, when the pain in my legs and my brain felt wrung like a wet sponge, there was also no one to share the moment with me and say, "Isn't suffering a little bit better when we suffer together?"

This is what the witch has done to me.

Love, beauty, and pain are best when shared.

It was the witch's work, but today I remain hopeful in my travels. I believe every curse has a way to be broken. And so I move. I went west, west, and further west, and ended up in the United States of America.

It's March 2022. 7 a.m. I'm unsure where I am. What I know for certain is that I'm sitting in the dirt on the side of a hill, overlooking a small town rousing from sleep, nestled in a valley. The golden morning is a beauty I hold close to my heart, and it is mine alone. And I say to it, "Isn't this the most wonderful thing on Earth you have ever seen?" The morning doesn't respond, although I hoped it would.

Later, I descend into the town and, because I haven't bathed since crossing the river three days ago, I smell like rotted apples, and my skin is caked in dirt. A few people on the sidewalk see me, and their faces contort with fear (or is it disgust?). Cars pass and the eyeballs inside follow me, asking without words, "What are you doing here in our town? Our Eden?"

As a cursed wanderer, I am used to the frowns, scrunched noses, and furled brows of those wondering what devilry this stranger will commit. I retreat to an alleyway between a hardware store and an abandoned building with the word *Seeds* painted in faded yellow on the side, and there is no one to say to me, "Don't worry about the locals, they do not know of what they judge so harshly."

No one to say, "Isn't suffering a little bit better when we suffer together?"

And I feel the witch's curse.

I sit on the oil-stained sidewalk amidst the rotten food and cardboard boxes and wait for the morning rush to pass, around 10 a.m., when the sidewalk and car traffic typically die down. But my stomach grumbles. When was the last time I ate?

After about an hour of wandering, I find the town's supermarket. Near the cart disposal and the exit doors, which open and close in a windy *whoosh*, I ask patrons if I can help carry their groceries for a dollar. Many shake their head "no." Not a single person responds with words, except for a small boy holding hands with his mother. He asks, "Why do people live outside?"

I nod, and the mother whisks him away. She switches her bag of groceries from one hand to the other, putting herself between the boy and me, as if I were dangerous. But I am not. The mother doesn't know that I once had a home, a wife, and everything I ever needed. She doesn't know I once ushered the spiders outside instead of killing them, even though my wife insisted I kill them because *what if the spiders come back inside?*

Did the German witch know of these memories?

No.

Did I? Where was this home from my memories now?

Swept away by the floods.

Where was this wife of my memory now?

Cancer took her to heaven, a place I no longer believed in.

But I believe she exists. Somewhere.

The mother knows none of this, and I can't blame her. She's not telepathic. No one is.

Why are we outside? I think, receiving a dollar from an old woman who refused to let me carry the 24-pack of water she was clearly struggling with. I still cannot afford bread.

Why do people live outside?

I was cursed on a random winter night, but I wonder if wandering was a destiny I chose. For the others who sleep outside, who have no choice, there are thousands of empty buildings across this country with the heat or the A/C on, bringing comfort to no one.

WHY!

In 2020, over 550,000 people experienced homelessness in the United States on a single night.

Resources exist. We have the money. We have the heart, the love that exists in balance with suffering.

Why has the curse of wandering alone affected so many?

This time my words are not in my head. I yell, *"FUCKING WHY DO WE LIVE OUTSIDE?"* and a man with round glasses and curly hair, carrying a brown paper bag with kale and a baguette poking out the top, runs to his car.

He stares at me while talking on his phone. He is calling the police, and I must go.

I risk arrest by moving to other places around town and continuing to beg, but I must eat. Such is the other, more tangible curse—the curse of hunger. After four hours of raising money, I can finally afford bread and return to the supermarket.

I leave this town and wander west to the next one. I climb the hills outside it and eat my bread in the dirt, watching the most beautiful sunset I have ever seen. Autumn is in the air. There is an electricity that comes from the friction created by rubbing love and suffering together, and everything, literally everything, gains an entire life behind it.

Perhaps this is what they mean by meaning?

Our pain. Our joy.

I wish I had someone to share these thoughts with me, but the curse goes on.

I don't know this now, but everything will soon change.

If only I could grab that setting sun with my index finger and my thumb and hold it above the horizon for a few seconds longer.

I ask the sun to come back.

But it doesn't respond.

Sun Come Back

I unfold the map on the hood of the car
I am lost
No idea where to go

And all around me the forest groans
As if the tall pines settle after a long day

I struggled to get here
Thousands of nights I traveled

Then smoke rises from the engine
Then all four tires catch fire

The airbags blow and the birds scatter
From their nests high up in the pines

When I hold my breath
The forest is silent
And it occurs to me

This map's no good
It never was
In fact it's the wrong map
It's not even a map

I look around
Turns out I wasn't even on a road

And that's not my car

Now the sun has gone red and
There are still hundreds of miles to go and

The road is dark and
The sky is dark and

I'm compelled to move
But I decide to sit and wait
Without fear or so I hope

I believe there is a happy ending here

And the sun
Will come back

I haven't been around enough to judge the people in this town

The only way to count the stars
is to let them fall from the sky
and count the property damage
in US dollars

It's to let the black holes
that pothole the asphalt
suck in all the houses
and send them away

To where it doesn't matter

I walk downtown like how
gravity keeps all the people from floating

Away

I now know
The only way to measure light
is to see it expand and contract and
breathe like a lung while I
Count time like grains of sand

I yearn to find you in the morning
Telling me where you traveled to
and for how long you stayed
(although you were never here
I continue to dream
I had the chance to say
goodbye)

I know I haven't been around enough
To judge the people of this town
But I know one day they'll become
Like all those falling stars

A Lime Love Story

The second time I fell in love
Occurred a little after
Seven in the evening
I was alone
Wandering and hungry
Not a thing to eat all day
A strip of bark here or there
A cup of dirt, deep-fried air
I had not an ounce of strength in me
I was exhausted
Creeping back to my kingdom woods
I was careful not to be seen
As usual
Traveling
Under the cover of dusk
With legs like sludge, up the moss hill
Under the rusty water tower
And its brown-red spider legs
Paint-stripped
With the town's name painted on the side
My body
Was eating itself
From the inside out
Faster I walked
Along the dark country roads
When I heard a rustle from a willow tree
A soft gnawing sound

That drew my attention
And upon closer inspection
I saw you
Nestled within the tree's snug arms
Which I brushed aside
You, eyes wide
A look of shock
A touch of shame
Your hands shielded
A brown paper grocery bag
That was overflowing with limes
And there were discarded rinds
Littering the dirt around you
There was even green juice
Flowing down your chin
Strands of pulp between your teeth
Like a deer, you froze
I crawled to you
Safe in that willow tree
Dried leaves crackled under my knees
As if I were being pulled to you
I told you not to be afraid
That I was only hungry
And possibly in love
And far from dismayed
Without a word
You laid out a lime
Which I took and
In return
I gave you a leaf
So you could wipe off the slime
Stuck to your chin
You said "Now I must go"

I took a large bite of your lime
I didn't want to eat alone
Softly you spoke
As if it wasn't for me to hear
"Please, please don't say a thing
This is my place. These are mine
Here, I can be without limes"
You handed me another
While I ate you smiled
And your lips
Silently mouthed the words
Now that's better, isn't it?
You gave me another and
I tore it to shreds
Lodging pulp in my teeth
Which was what you did when
I noticed you
Doing the same
And I couldn't believe
How we were covered in limes
And I said
"I'm sorry"
Which you replied
"Don't be, but now it's time
I really must go"
"But I'll wait for you here"
"And I'll never come back
And you're far too kind"
I watched you leave the willow tree
Moving through its branches like a door
To another world
One without hunger
Because you left me

Your brown paper grocery bag
Overflowing with limes
Which I took with me
Under the water tower
Down the moss hill
Back into my woods
Held in my mind
You, I would never see
Again

Secret blue underwear

After dusk comes dawn
With no night between

You roll over
Half asleep
You look at me
Words like cigarettes you ask

Is it day
Or is it night

My throat is dry
I can't say
Maybe both
Then again
Perhaps neither

We decide there is
Nothing between
Because whatever this is
Is right

Verdigris in exile

Who would have guessed
That the tiny geriatric in me would piss off
The zealots of this town
The ones who claim I am a stalker
(A claim unfounded)
The town that delivers swift deliberation
With hot spit and four-syllable words
They say they have their rules
Laws cooked on the spot
they say
You cannot come here
You cannot interfere with half the town
"Peeping in our cottages"
(sick! they say)
"Following us in our streets"
they say
They've seen me taking notes
On how they come and go
And they say I follow far too close
That I breathe on their necks
they say
They say now is the time for me to go

But maybe my ears don't hear too well
My mind operates like static
Plus their voices mutter underwater
Where downpouring rain drowns all sound

I am the first to admit my attention is wrought
I step back from my judge, hands up: "I'll go"
I'm leaving
"And I will never come back again"

Then I go
Or I pretend to
but no
It's this lie I've told
It's the two fingers crossed
(hugging)
behind my back
I can't go
I won't
Their town has conquered my heart
Some people are good
The ones not so pissed
Between the cracks
There is kindness here
And I can relax

So I forgo their exile
I raise my tiny geriatric middle finger
On my walk to the edge of town
I raise the other as I turn around
And return
Dressed as an unhoused creature in a cape of blankets
And a caterpillar mustache
On the sidewalk, I beg
A dollar or two and wish for the best
I get a dime and I'm blessed
In the park I lay my head and rest
I tune myself to the night's cold touch

To how the evening clouds turn red
and
I wake up under a blanket
and
I remember
How the kindness of this town
Climbs out of bed

I smile at a man
Who stares at me from his car
"You there" he says
His words float through the air
He cracks a laugh and says
"Whatever, God bless"

And I don't mind my exile here
As if I had never left

The moon watches overhead
I wander alongside a chain-link fence
Of the empty playground
Full of rust and a story of
Life before death

A couple lies on the grass
Watching the stars overhead

Before midnight I go to the corner store
Where its neon lights buzz white noise
Inside I ask if a dime is enough for coffee
The woman behind the counter tells me
It's free
As long as I pay her a memory

Which she pays first
She tells me of her mother
And how every Sunday
They met for lunch at a diner

I think about this
I tell her how the best memories
Make you
You

I tell her of a memory that hasn't happened yet
How we climbed to the roof
Of a neon light and white noise
Corner store
To stargaze

Like a couple in the park

Climb we must
For the memories we create
Before they crumble to dust
I tell the woman: I find it hard to leave your town
Because there is love here
There is kindness here
Which, these days, can be hard to find

The next morning I walk between
Warehouses in a sea of concrete
Wrapped in my blanket
Holed shoes shuffling through the streets
I return to the council where
The zealots no longer have mouths
Their heads fused together

They stare at the ceiling
Lost in thought

Lost in their memories

I can't look away from the horror I see
Until one sees me

He shifts in his chair and huffs through his nose
I believe he says
This town
Is the City of God
You, bum, you are too odd
You are a fraud
We have no place for you here
You are disease
Fear incarnate

The definition of disgust

Because of you
We're forced to see
Life on the street
The ugliness of our ways
What we do to you
What you do to
This town

What have I done—I ask
The present will burn in our memories

I left the zealots in their non-verbal daydream
I went to the garden to plant a seed

New memories
Like weeds popping up in all your pretty lawns

I say—louder, bolder
You cannot take me from here
You cannot change the way I'm me
You cannot slow my life down
You cannot thaw my verdigris

You cannot do anything
—to me

Nuclear Weapon, Night Light

The light turns pink at the sound of the bells
I move slowly over a patch of fresh-cut grass
A park I don't know the name of
I find a bench where I can sit

In front of me are golden elms
Wafting in the evening breeze
To me, it seems, we have nowhere to go

And when I think about it

We have nothing to do
We have nothing to be

This is how the panic seeps in
A panic like broken glass
I focus on the hardwood of the bench where I sit
I inspect the rows of elms, drifting like breathing
The sky is ultraviolet and growing dark and bright
I see it consuming our town

Now the calm rushes over me
Like a wave
Because I hear
Wind whistling
Taxis that accelerate and honk
Dogs that call in the night

I realize this park is
Without a name

I would have stayed here forever
I would have made myself a home
But then you came along
To sit next to me
To ask me to close my eyes
To think of my home, jangling my keys
You take my watch, shoes, the jacket I wear
The latter of which hangs to your toes
So I, restless,
Have something to do
I move slowly
Where the light turns nuclear pink
Slowly

Home

Letter from the Trash #1

Springtime, late afternoon.

I'm standing in a grass meadow spotted yellow with dandelions. The horizon is flat; there are no hills here. No edges. Large puffy clouds move like bugs across the landscape where the meadow touches the sky. In my eyes, the sunlight blurs, leaving a haze that bleeds as far as I can see. I wonder: *Have I come to heaven?* How did I get here? I try to remember. What is all this? *Why does it feel outside my grasp? Elusive.*

I stick out my tongue, and a ten-limbed creature with eyes at the end of its antennae crawls out of my throat, leaves a dollop of syrup on my tongue, and jumps to the ground. The alien thing from within me burrows beneath the surface, laughing as it crawls and fades away. The creature is gone as quickly as it came.

I sit and close my eyes and wait for my life to be over. When I open them again, the meadow is gone, but in its place is a home. I have no choice but to enter, pulled by a tractor beam. The home is not from my childhood or any other period in my life. It's not a place I've seen or visited before. I do not recognize the rooms inside. The floorboards are made of a mystery material that's not quite wood but wood-adjacent, and the dusty stairwell leads to shadows and unknowns above.

Where is this world taking me? Meadows? Homes? I have no control here and wander about its empty rooms. The floor creaks and moans with each step—the only sound I hear. In the linoleum kitchen, there is a window, and when I look outside, there is a tree with leaves that flutter from a nonexistent wind. Beyond it, a void. Black. More nothing.

I'm getting tired of this.

I need clarity. I need all this to make sense.

Life won't pass any faster, so I must fill my time.

My fear travels from one world to another.

I close my eyes and hear a radio blaring my favorite song. I open my eyes—and I am the song.

Notes tacked to the lines on musical tablature. I don't like this, and it hurts.

I fall into a pure void. Pure annoyance.

How did it know? How did I get here?

Where am I going?

WHY!

WHY CAN'T I GO BACK IN TIME WHEN EVERYONE WAS ALIVE?

Everything's changing again.

Life is too long; life is too short.

The fear deepens.

Do you hear me? Do you read my words? LEAVE THIS TOWN. LEAVE IT NOW.

I hear the sounds of a lawnmower, but I can't pinpoint where the sound originates. In this new place, there are no houses, no overgrown lawns of Kentucky grass to render pristine. There are no people even to operate the mower. So where does this mowing sound come from? A memory of summer Saturdays? Fuck that. It comes from the void.

I look up and see the giant bug-clouds again on a backdrop of black; there are multiple voids in the distance. Not even a horizon wants to be here.

I taste poison in the air. I say a swear word, but it's bleeped out.

This town is child-friendly, I guess.

As I continue through it on the journey of my life, I recognize no places, no faces.

I remember: it's springtime, late afternoon—and I should be grateful.

But how will I pass the time? All I've done is done and cannot be fixed.

Once the sun goes beyond the horizon here, there is no pulling it back.

I repeat: THERE IS NO PULLING IT BACK.

LEAVE NOW.

Signed: Catania, August 2022

A Downtown Love Story

I remember the day
The temperature was a degree above freezing
Pre-winter rain falling downtown
It had been falling all morning
From the ashen clouds

Moments earlier I finished my breakfast
Eggs and toast and coffee
Smidge of bacon
Over at the diner on the corner
Washington Park

I was leaning against a brick wall
Hiding from the rain, solace beneath the eaves
Gazing out at the embrace of a freezing fall day
Somewhere near 34th and 8th
I was gnawing on the filter of a menthol cigarette
Smoking between my lips
Between sips of gin and ginger beer
I was working
My job: to keep folks safe
To keep the peace
I'm a superhero
Unofficially at least
But that's when I overheard you say
To a man holding your hand

"If you make me a smoothie
You'll mold me like clay"

The man grinned
His lips unfurled. Mr. Secret Whisper
With cheeks that stretched to the graying sky
"Shall we do it at my place?
At least we'll get out of this rain"
One of your eyebrows jumped up, you said
"You know the mail won't come today
I told you. The postman is away"

I was drenched to the bone
Every fiber in me shivered
I could not understand what you meant
I did not follow this need
I yearned to get just a little bit closer
I yearned like I bleed
But then I tripped and stumbled off the curb and
My menthol cigarette
Landed in a puddle in the gutter and
My half-pint of gin shattered and
Pieces of glass lodged into my neck
And like that
I bleed

Luckily, you saw none of this
The pre-winter rain washed away the blood
Muted my disgrace
I stood and lit another cigarette
Smoked half of it
Smoke billowing out my neck hole
Watching you and the man
As you window-shopped

When we passed the TV store
There was a news reporter
Who said, "That's it, folks—there's just no way"
He abandoned his desk and I could hear
Off camera
"What? There's no longer anything to say"

I laughed because
Fifty-ish steps behind you and the man
All I could think of was what I would say

Later we arrived at what I assumed
Was your brownstone home
I was watching through the ground-floor window
I could see him standing in the kitchen
In nothing but a towel around his waist
Rummaging through the fridge
I was hidden in the shadows outside
The rain-soaked air that muted all light
Raindrops, heavier than mercury
Running down the glass like droplets of silver
Footsteps approaching
Then I heard a creak

Quickly I dived behind a boxwood
Just as the front door swung open
And I saw you leave, alone
You hoisted your jeans and you popped an umbrella
And disappeared into the freezing rain

The storm grew violent
Wind like ice cut into my face
I followed you as close as I could

Weaving and pushing through
The rush hour crowds on the sidewalk
The folks I unofficially swore to protect
But in an instant I lost sight of you
And like that—you were gone
No more

I sat in a flood in the gutter and cried
Because I didn't even catch your name
I cried because there will be a day
When I'll forget your face
Like my reflection in the puddle at my feet
You will blur
Affected by ripples
And become vague

From that moment on, you blurred
Slowly, day by day
Until
Many years later
I was smoking a menthol against a wall downtown
I had just finished my breakfast
Eggs and toast and coffee
Smidge of bacon
Gin and ginger beer
The superhero way
This time there was a clear blue sky
This pre-winter October day
All I did was get high
And walk
Looking in the brownstones

Around noon I found it
Near the mills on the eastern side of town
Imagine my surprise
After all this time
The building from a storybook
With evenly spaced, orderly windows
A heavy wooden door
Vines that crawled from planters between the stairs
A light pole out front, arms half-mast
Holding little yellow lights
I remembered none of this the first time
Except the boxwood where I hid
Jumping to a ledge, I grasped
I pulled myself to the living room window
Inside I saw you
Dancing
My eyes nearly melted from the shock
I thought I would never see you again
But now
Hanging on your ledge
For a moment
Listening to the very same music as you
I felt every beat of my heart
It had been so long
Since I followed you
On that pre-winter rainy day
Your long hair was now even longer
And when you spun in circles
Like a top
It wrapped around you
Surrounded you and held you
Like a letter in an envelope
As you spun and spun

And then you stopped
Because I believe you saw me too

The hair fell flat against your back
One hand flew across your naked breasts
The other between your pressed thighs
Another crept over your bare skin shoulder
Another tickled your neck
Another came through your legs
And I saw your head fall back
Three more ran through your hair
Hands everywhere
Two lifted you by the bottoms of your feet
Hands caressing your ears
Taking the utmost care
Lightly running down your forearm
You were exalted
All the while
I, melting
Out on the ledge
The cigarette smoke burning
The gin burning
My eyes

It was then I discovered
That I
Was the ghost in the window
Who needed to disappear

Another year passed
October rolled around again
I stood on the corner like a maple tree
With my bare branches raised

My roots dug firmly in the dirt
I could hear everything everyone said
The people I swore to protect
Superhero me
I could see everything everyone could see
The tips of my branches full of menthol cigarettes
My roots drinking the autumn pre-winter gin
And no harm could reach me

It was there I could think

Again a year would pass before I moved from that spot
Finally ready to see you
I needed to be near you
So I transformed into a candle that sat in your window
Of that beautiful brownstone
Every night when the rain was light
You could set my wick on fire
In the morning, in the evening
Every weekend, every weekday
I, lit
And I could wave with the breeze
My flame warming your air
Around me and eventually
You

And me? The real me?
For you, I was the sky of autumn blue
For you, I was a pre-winter rain
I was trees
Cigarettes
Candles, too
I was music

Guitars and pianos
Sounds with and without words
Everything

You were the world and I was
Everything

And I remember
How absurd I looked
How you hooked me
So one day
You could make me into a smoothie
And you could mold me like clay

Leave me alone on this terrible, horrible night

Thanks to my veins preserved with ice
I now have hair full of worms and lice
It's this body that made the night still
The head's violent shaking until thoughts spill

Days have a taste and to me they taste like ick
If I taste myself I taste like fish
Unlike you and your menthol cream
You who latch onto every dream

Thanks to my room empty except for pink curtains
Thanks to all these sermons about virgins
I am an icebox of market-price fish
Drifting down the river into the ancient abyss

Is this life of mine a wasted dream
Where goodbyes sound like your menthol cream
I am a fish skedaddling to the sea
Is this life the taste of you and me

Thanks to a love stroke in a wine pool
Thanks to the night that only has one rule
A ladder with steps to the bright room
The fog in the streetlights spells doom

I'm on the pier in a box of ice
A head as raucous as worms and lice
The sea that's laced with menthol cream
And you who latch onto my every dream

A guide to local culture

One day I hope
I will find you in the kitchen
Talking on the phone
With the door wide open
Your voice in every room of the house
Your body framed in the door
A ghost, reflected in the glass

But for now
I wait until the sirens come
I look until I hear their words
"My God, what happened here?"
I hear the other one say,
"It was some kind of beast,
A monster, I don't know. Something more."
The first one looks at me and replies,
"Jesus. My God."

I swore to them I meant no harm
I show them that I have twigs for arms
Which I raise to the sky
And demonstrate how I can
Pick up the TV signal
This should be enough
They should know there is nothing to fear

I take a step forward, stupid yet bold
I ask where they're from, what they adore

When 15 bullets fly, metallic and cold

Then 15 more

I hear:
"Die you monster!"
"Satan's whore."

I count the holes
I ask, "What have you done?"
Into the floor I crash
Through the earth I fall
Until
Like you, reflected in the glass

Who Goes On an Adventure: A Biography

In the late 1980s, a custard boy became self-aware in the rural cheese town of Brodhead, Wisconsin. Among the gentle hills and dairy farms, the boy came to a sudden realization of his existence, of space and time, of consciousness, and with it were images of Santa and God and clothes from American Eagle. Consciousness opened his eyes in the same violent manner that one takes a baseball to the face. It was all violence and cheese and sport.

Epiphany #1.

When consciousness came, the boy was playing with his friends in the wooden corridors beneath wooden steeples and plastic slides of the town's cheese-themed playground. *Where am I?* he wondered, suddenly more alive than ever. *How did I get here? Am I alive? Does that mean I will die?*

The custard boy looked at his friends. Two of the three boys also came into consciousness at the playground around the same time, and the two girls who were also playing there experienced their versions of coming-into-being over breakfast that morning. For all four, consciousness was rendered palpable. It was like they were all shocked by lightning and re-transplanted to an alien planet.

"What is this place?" one boy thought. "What the Buddy Holly hell is this?"

One of the girls used her thoughts to scream.

The other boy said he needed a gun to protect himself and his family from the government.

The rural custard boy attempted to control his thoughts but sent them into the mind of one of the girls by accident. She turned away and crossed her arms, and she never spoke to the custard boy again.

The remaining boy, the yet-unconscious one, was unaware of what was happening to his friends, and instead he dug his hands and feet into the wood chips. He would gain his own consciousness a few weeks later, when he walked in on his parents naked and fighting under the bedsheets. Trauma and being: it would define the boy's life.

These now-conscious boys and girls of cornland America planted their roots in the cheese-themed schools with the cheese and mice mascots that championed their football and basketball teams. Everything mattered then; equally, they sucked in Americana dreams like vanilla milkshakes sucked through plastic straws. They were cheese trees that spoke and moved. Their branches sprouted from their heads like maples and birches in spring. Every October, they flowered and their leaves fell, and they stood bare, exposed for the brittle winter.

Such is life in cheeseland.

When he was ten, the rural custard boy and his two brothers joined the neighbor kids and built a corn palace for their cheese reign. But who would be king? they wondered. Now was not the time for violence, but to crown the head cheese, they donned armor and cried, "King of the Mountain!" and pushed one another off the Native burial mounds in the trees behind their houses. The king was dethroned at least three times a week. With the right amount of violence, the custard boy knew he could be king.

When summer blazed and lingered with its thick, breathless humidity, the kids jumped on the trampolines of the rich kids and picked crayfish out of the river. When the boy was fourteen, he discovered everyone was touching each other all summer long. Naked pre-teen bodies jumped through sprinklers and biked to the swimming pool. They stole candy and hot dogs from the gas station next to the bowling alley. Later, they'd retreat to the wood-paneled basements to discover weed and alcohol and touch each other while watching movies on mute on TV.

During those summers, they were baptized in the lakes and rivers dotting and cutting through the southern Wisconsin hills. The rural custard boy's younger brother nearly drowned once. The custard boy mistook his younger brother's angelic blonde hairs, floating near the surface, for a fish.

"Hey! A fish!"

Their mother screamed and dived in, pulling the younger brother from the water, crying and kissing the skin off his body.

Autumn was the preferred season for the custard boy. Life made sense under those gray October skies. The body felt good shivering inside a hoodie. He could smell rain in the air even when the sidewalks were dry. On cooler days, he walked the trail behind the hardware store, through woods to a small pond surrounded by scores of cattails sticking out of the shallow water and bullfrogs croaking from hidden hideouts. The custard boy listened.

The moon watched the boy sitting on the shore; the boy watched the moon.

"There are people who are not me," the custard boy said.

He sounded sad, the moon later reported.

Epiphany #2.

"What's happening out there? Everything! There are so many people, so many places, so much to do; everything must be happening all at once! And yet nothing happens to me!"

The moon listened to the custard boy's evening laments for years.

When he was sixteen, the rural custard boy and his friends broke into his grandparents' house on the other side of town. The *nicer* side of town. Near the golf course, where the doctors lived. *Pill Hill.*

With his grandparents wintering in Phoenix, they'd stolen the garage door opener and parked inside to stay hidden. They had free rein. The neighbors never knew. They'd head straight to the basement, drink the grandparents' liquor, and play pool by throwing the pool balls with their hands as hard as they could, damaging the green felt and trying to smash their fingers.

Years earlier, when he was eleven, the custard boy and his brothers were left in the 1970s-era basement of the town's only bank while their mom worked upstairs. It was in this basement that they could spend hours staring at a picture on the wall of a woman in a wet, translucent T-shirt. The shirt only covered 60 percent of her breasts.

It was then that the custard boy *awakened*!

That same year, the custard boy saw the movie Titanic in theaters, on the ultra-large silver screen. He saw Rose undress and slap her hand against the foggy window of a 1912 Renault Type CB Coupé de Ville. The boy: *awaken, again!*

Epiphany #3.

Today, the custard boy is a hedonist.

As an adult, he adores rubber clothes.

When he goes on an adventure it is sex sex sex until history loses all meaning. Cheese-themed parks and schools. Mice mascots. Kings of the hills. Dead brother fish. The woman in the basement. Until history is frozen. A postcard of the past.

The custard boy has left the cheese land. He is awake like everyone else. Conscious all the time.

Emergency!

At least now I'm certain
There is a mood I can't define
That comes like a cloud into all our lives

The sirens oscillate in every city center
Beetle-like movements of a thousand ambulances
Wailing all day and night

I try to understand what's happening outside
Why the town has become empty
Why does everyone everywhere hide

There is a collective shiver from
A cold and sickly wind
That creeps in broad daylight

Today I live in bunker time
The words on the wires say it's okay
They say the morning will come

But when I look
The night sky is starless
And the moon has gone

And it's the same
Everywhere
For everyone

They see the frost is misty
That hangs on the hospital glass
Between us

What is this place

Between two mountains I walk for weeks
Through the black forest along a paper-thin trail
My feet are blistered, my hands charred and sore
But on I walk
Until one day
My legs as thin as twigs snap like sticks
And I dare not take a step more

Thus I fall
Into the dirt and
I crawl
Deeper into the valley and

I crawl
On and on along the forest floor
Shadows as if the sun never was
Encircled by knife-wielding trees
Jabbing and slicing at me
Thorns grow from the ground
Crowning me
Calling me their king
I tell them I am only passing through
That I am nothing
I am not their king
That I don't know anything

Then I hear the wind as a chorus of whispers
Adjacent to my trail
They lay a moss carpet before me
And a god-like voice booms "Go!"
I see the eye, carved into a great oak tree
Look to the sky
In prayer

I ask the tree
Am I a king
Or a tourist
Of this forest?
Me?

Through the thicket
At the end of the moss carpet
Is a throne

Never before have I yearned
For anything
To have nothing
Never before have I frothed at the mouth
To desire the forest
And devour its gaze

Hence the trap I fell into
My body seeps into the moss like dew
Roots appear and wrap around my ankles
Roots grip my wrists and
Pull me beneath the dirt, out of view

And in the depths below
I hurt

I fall
This forest has taken me
It has given me a choice
Between death and omnipotence
Bones or saturation
I could grace the throne
And this forest would be
Mine

Yet in the depths below the forest floor
I hurt
Sinking, yearning for more
No longer are my feet blistered
No longer are my hands charred and sore
I am sinking into the underground
All the way through
Until I come through
The surface on the other side

I am changed, transformed
I am the knife-wielding tree
I am integral to me
My roots extend for miles
Searching the forest for what I cannot see

I spread like wildfire, until
I arrive at a cottage made of birch trees
And a stone chimney
Burping up smoke
Wood-trimmed windows and bent glass
Doors painted a forest black
I move across the lawn
Through the coconut bedsheets drying on the line

Walk up on the porch
Between pots of green and red wildflowers
A wagon wheel leaning against the wall

What is this place? I wonder
And could I make it mine?

Because the forest is mine
For I wear a crown
The cottage, too, must be mine
But the cottage is also a home
The place I miss most

These roots of the underground
Crawling, they cover
Every inch of this home
Crawling up those cottage walls

I see through the window
Frosted by the coming winter
Which is only a few weeks away

Inside, I see you
You: lying across a couch
You: legs akimbo
One foot on the floor

I think about how
I had been walking for weeks
And my roots are pining for something
To prove I'm the king
Of the overground

But when I see you
Everything goes away

My roots are sucked into my chest
Like dust in a vacuum

From the window I adore you
I am full of words to say to you
But what I croak was a meek
Help me
Save me
Let me
Stay
In this place
Away from the forest
Where I am lost
Where I am promised to be king

Here with you I can
Be
Anything

I tap on your windowsill
Tapping until your body shakes
As if in your dreams
You fell backwards off a chair
You found yourself in freefall
For a second
But on you sleep
And on I stare
I listen to your snores like
Someone mowing the lawn
On a spring Sunday morning

Then out of a pitch-black shadow
From an oak tree behind the cottage
Comes a whisper that says

"You better believe if you wake her
If you interrupt her sleep
I'll need you to be running
For she'll be throwing stones
That fly a hundred miles an hour
That cut through the air
That'll cut through you like firewood."

I scoff, "You don't understand!
You don't understand a thing!
Up there
I am the forest and I am its king!
Here, I love her."
I say, louder this time
"What I should do *is* everything!

I will wake whoever I please."

The shadow steps into
The sickly pale porchlight
And I see
A woman with hair like spiders
With a voice like dirty snow

"I said!" she said.
"Wake her and you better go!"

On the window I tap
Wake up wake up wake up

49

Tappity tap TAP!

Inside the cottage
I see your body stir
You bolt upright
Bursting from a dream
Sleep falling from your hair

The spider-haired woman frowns and says
"Oh, you've done it now.
Time to go.
Time to run!"

I tap tap I TAPPITY TAP TAP!

"I will not run!" I say
And—*snap!*
The shadow woman takes my knife-tipped root
And snaps it in half
She bends it until it breaks
Looking me in the eye
Her own are blue like glacier ice
Psychotic and wide

Inside

I see you kneeling in the corner
I see the hate on your face
Stolen from sleep's grace
You gather your rocks
For hundred-mile-an-hour throws
One rock after the other
They blow the shutters right off

Cracks the size of a canyon
Grow across your walls

I look at the liminal woman
She is as scared as I
And, together
We say,
"Run."

I do not make it far
Your lightning rocks
Catch up with me and
Remind me of pain and
Return me to the dirt
From where I came

When you catch up to me
You hack my roots to bits
You say, "You are a king of nothing."
I tell you, "I am sorry for waking you."
I explain how I need you
How I need you to need me
To come with me
To my home above ground
Where you can sleep
As long as you liked

The spider-haired woman
Carries my broken roots
In a canvas bag
She says I didn't realize
What my actions said

That evening
My bones are used as
The warmth in her fireplace
My smoke rises through the chimney
I do not stop at the sky
I rise through it
But before I leave
I look down
At what I assume is
The cottage where you live
And all I want to know is
Who you were
And where you learned to throw
Those hundred-mile stones
Where did you go
And what is this place
That made you
You

Advertisement: unsettling music plays

I was wandering one cold October night
I looked up and saw a billboard
That made me shake
Like sweet violent confusion
The ad went a little something like this:

There exists a beater frog
Who gets off beating the raven
Because of what God was doing to its feed
Because the blue moon was high above them
Slobbering with greed
The raven caws
This bird out of time
Out comes the beater frog's jaw
Hung open in the nightmare face
The slogan: A home with no food
Is no home to embrace

I said to me: you are a tramp man
You are not the one they seek
This dream of the perfect home
Was not made for me
For I be the one who wanders
I can survive the cold
On I go on, onto the next ad
Which went a little something like this:

There is a lavatory on the right
And you have no time to spare
A blue moon is eating the light
Full of the knowledge that
You will never make it there
The floor is rife with a murder of crows
The sky is green and your pain shows
The slogan: get a life, go below

I said to myself: maybe these ads
Are just a show
Not made for me

Letter from the Trash #2

Anything with a beginning will end.

This truism was a constant reminder she carried throughout her life, from the early days of puberty. She applied the concept in work, relationships, dinners, positive emotions, and even sunsets. No matter what it was, she knew it all would end. Nothing was permanent. Everything temporary. This was especially true when it came to the sensations brought about by her heaven's tour guide of cannabis and opium, her favorite ways to pass the time, but horribly temporary.

Time, too, she knew, would end. One day.

She sat on the balcony of their shared apartment on Amsterdam's western side, looking down upon the overgrown courtyard. A period of her life was ending precisely because it began. She couldn't get the idea of impermanence out of her mind.

It was a little past ten in the evening, and the August sun dipped behind the row of connected brick apartment buildings across the courtyard. The building opposite looked like a wall with windows in perfect order. Within these windows, which were wide open to view inside and never obstructed by blinds or anything else, she watched the people move about their evenings. Cooking dinner. Smoking out the open window. Watering plants. Naked yoga. Many windows were open because it wasn't raining, which, for August in Amsterdam, was a rare event. The soft cool breeze also meant there was a reprieve from the humidity.

She sat outside in a t-shirt for the first time that year. It was good to let her skin breathe, even if only for a Dutch sunset. A hand-rolled spliff sagged from her lips. The tobacco dizzied her brain; the marijuana pulled and stretched it like laffy taffy. The most common moments of morphineland are the moments without morphine, which she smoked an hour before off a piece of tin foil. The plume of light-blue smoke from her spliff was rising into the air. Her girlfriend watched her through the kitchen window. She saw the smoke curl and disappear, and she tried not to think about how their relationship was ending. She was changing; they were changing.

Beginning, ending.

The sky was glowing red, a solid sheet of color rising from the rooftops like waves of smoke. The spliff burned into the filter and she spat the butt out. It landed in the green courtyard and smoldered underneath a bushel of overgrown weeds.

She mentioned her favorite word was *mierenneuker*. Ant fucker.

Who is the *real* antfucker?

They were ending. She was ending. The sunset was ending.

The sky faded from its red color to a solid blue, then purple, and then black. No stars. Just pure black. Another day was gone. Another day would eventually begin, carried by the morning, but she had no hope of seeing it in the way she imagined it. It would be a surprise for better or worse.

A surprise that would end.

But then it occurred to her—normally, the sky leaves the day faster than the sun allows. This evening, the sky went from light blue to pitch black in what felt like seconds. How was this possible? What nonsense was that? Darkness had descended as if someone had thrown a blanket over Amsterdam.

That wasn't how the sky worked.

Not then. Not now.

She figured every Dutch person in the country must have noticed it.

"The only thing that's free is the sunrise," she remembered her girlfriend saying about Dutch skies.

What about the sudden onset of night? Was that free too?

Her girlfriend joined her on the balcony.

"Did you see that?" she asked. She could hear a tint of panic in her voice.

"See what?" She flicked on her lighter, lit a cigarette, and passed it to her girlfriend. She had a book in her lap, which she opened and began to read using a square of light coming from the kitchen.

"How is it?" she asked, forgetting about the sky. Maybe she was too high. Maybe she didn't know what to say.

"Shh, shh," the girlfriend responded. Even when she *shushed* her, her presence made the air feel lighter. She couldn't remember how they fell in love, why she once loved her. Memories gone. Perhaps this was why it was ending.

She read her book and plopped her feet on her lap. She sweated in fear. The sun had disappeared. The sky went black in the most unnatural way, and now anxiety was consuming her. The sky will come back, right? Her memories harbored a film of cloudy milk over them. No rose glasses here. She was in trouble. Not a single damn memory.

"I can hear you thinking," the girlfriend said with a sigh. The book slammed shut. "It's very distracting, you know."

Ended end end end.

"Sorry."

Sorry? Sorry! By God, what does it mean to be human if one can't think without irritating others?

"No sorries needed," she said. "But try not to think so loudly. Okay? Thank you. Love you."

Were they ending?

Had she broken up with her?

She attempted to calm her thoughts. She focused on the sounds coming from the apartments across the courtyard. Dishes clanged as they were cleaned. Music (Bob Marley). A row of laughter. She watched the Amsterdammers go about their nightly routines in the windows. She attempted to flush her mind like a toilet and erase her thoughts. Be dark like the sky. Be like the day and end!

"You're still thinking. Why are you trying to distract me? For heaven's sake, if you want to keep bothering me, could you do it without all this philosophizing?" The girlfriend rose from her chair in the same way that a human commits violence and stormed into the apartment. "It's just so loud!" she said, slamming the sliding door behind her.

She continued to sit, unmoving, stunned by the revelation. She could feel a light behind her eyes, faint yet growing brighter. She was beginning. She was ending. She was a sunset that would turn into a morning.

Signed: Amsterdam, August 2022

Code Red, 10 p.m.

I heard them saying it
They said

BURN, MONSTER MAN

BURN IT TO THE GROUND

Be like dry leaves
BE CRISPY AND BROWN

Be like the lake
BE THE RIPPLES IN THE WATER

RISE TO THE SKY
Rise like a helium balloon

COME, MONSTER MAN
Burn like the candles—blue

How to Save the Planet

Tonight I transform
Into a honey bee
So I can find myself
On the inside of

A paper cup
Wrapped in cellophane

I ask how did I get here
I buzz my escape

But I know
I'm trapped
And I know
I could die

Then again
If I'm let free
I may snap
And attack
Everyone around me

In this case
I will die

Like how everyone dies
How we all go extinct

Me the little honey bee
I see
You remove the cellophane
I sharpen my stinger
Ready to flee

I'm Homeless: So Don't Break Into My House

In this dollhouse of a body
You will pass a hundred thousand rooms
And three hundred thousand ways
To understand how plants bloom

There are hallways full of smoke
That strangle like soft weak hands
From the bonfires in each room
Letting their embers fly upward
Filling each nook with ash
The bonfires caused by oversized mirrors
That refract onto gasoline grass

In this dollhouse of a body
Wind-battered eyes blink like
Windows of porcelain snow
Curtains stained nicotine-yellow
Rows of doors the colors of sunset

To avoid the smoke you're advised to crawl
Down the halls with the doors painted blue
Don't peek into memories of a childhood bedroom
Follow the stairs alongside the ears
To the garden with two holes for a nose
Within a library of notes
And a telescope pointed north

In this dollhouse of a body
You explore its hundred thousand rooms
But you're pulled apart like a flower
Slapped until smoke comes out
For you'll burn for just a little bit longer

Instead the best way is out
Before the dolls come home
Slurring words like hello and welcome
They'll compel you to stay
They've painted it red
Over the sound of crackling wood
Not a word was said

In this dollhouse of a body
Let yourself free and wander the rooms
Open like a flower
Away from the bonfires
A dollhouse burning for a little bit longer

11 o'clock at night

The night drags on,
I wonder,
When did it become this long?
I have to count it with grains of sand.
I have to watch and count
Every spin of the ceiling fan.

Unable to sleep,
I escape to the diner,
Take a booth by the window and watch
The cars and people hobbling through the rain.
Besides the cook and a waitress,
I was the only one there, so
I lay my head on my hands and rest on the table.
I close my eyes and
Imagine I lived a life underwater.

But then,
I sink into the booth,

And I'm falling.
I've left my place at the diner,
I'm falling into a spaceship.
That takes me far away.

Eventually I land in an unearthly place.
A city that moves at lightning's pace.
A city where none of the stars shine
With streets of neon, and
Streets that eat and dance and grieve.

In my dream, I
Find a place selling noodles,
I sit on the curb and eat,
The day cured,
A woman runs and takes off to the skies
A man flickers
As if he were a trick to the eyes.

And, suddenly, the ship takes off again.
It takes me away.

To a more unbearable land,
Inside a hot oven with a salted Virginian ham.
I'm bread wrapped in tin foil,
Frying and burning a tarry black.
I bubble like oil.
Beetle black.

Then away I sail
On my space river of dreams.

Or I awake, absorbed
By the glow
Of neon outside.

The night drags on.
The diner is empty until morning.
I lean on the table,
I close my eyes until morning.

And I reassemble.

I won't wait
For the sun to rise.

I lay
My head down
Until it becomes the road
Where
Dreams show the way.

A man who lives in a cupola

You heard the story
Of the man
Who lives in a cupola
On top of the old clock tower
In a small Italian town
You've never heard of
A word that sounds like placenta

This man—said the papers
Was shouting, in English
"Fuck you!"
At no one
He had nothing but curses for the world
Blasphemy given up to the sky
Until another Italian man didn't understand
And cried back, in English
"Fuck me? Fuck you!"

The man in the cupola climbed down
Grunting, swatting at ghosts
Telling everyone to go away
He walked up the road
Shook his fist at the sky
And stood at the corner
Where he caught a bus
and never returned

The later I get, the more I forget

Remember a time long past
When the sun was as flat as a paper circle
When it wasn't as necessary as it is today
For all life on earth
If you don't believe it—
pull on them thought strings
Remember how it was
The child, unbridled
Who sat by the window in school
On those early autumn mornings
Gray skies, golden leaves in their trees
Only with eyes closed will it come to life
Clouds like dirty cotton as far as forever
A chill on the skin, a blanket, an embrace
To keep you warm
Warm like a memory
A memory when
You drew the sun with black sunglasses
A yellow circle with triangles around it
You drew how the sun broke through
The gray autumn skies
To illuminate your square blue house
Crudely rendered
With a pointed red roof
On it were three squares with crosses for windows
A singular cloud-like tree out front
And three stick figures holding hands

Two tall, one small
Words big and bold
"Me and My Family"
A warm memory
Which will only fade
When the end of life kicks in
And you have to remember
The sun is a sphere
Destined to move
Wearing sunglasses in space
The sun is to fear!
Always watching you wherever you go
Every day, every week
Months and years
Begging you to remember
That sunflowers are circles
Surrounded by triangles
Moving to face the sun
Making space for rainbows
Stretched between the gray autumn clouds
There's a child, unbridled
Who sat by the window in school
Making memories that fade
But won't go away
As long as you remember
The sun is as flat
As a paper circle

If you're scared, just hope

When the night is darkest
I shriek and destroy
Venturing outside
To shake my fist and
Say to the moon
You better go back down
You better turn off that light and
You better leave us alone
I compel it to go
Conjure spells to send it home
You gotta get outta here
Go back beneath the horizon
Go back to where you're darkest
These are the things I ask the moon
And I'm surprised
When all it does is refuse
Never have I heard such arrogance before
The moon is shouting back
Mocking me, cackling
Look at you
You!
You with your roof over your head
You with your bed to sleep in
I say, yes
Once in a while
I have a place to sleep
There might just be a bite to eat

Too
Confess, confess!
Okay—I cry
I said I want to rest
To be here when
The sun comes up and
The morning is orange in the east and
Quiet, I leave
Because I'm going west with
A face covered
For that fish to swim around my head
Baked in moonlight
A log where I can sit
A bridge my duty to mend
A day I imagine is coming to me

Yes, you see
The moon, disturbed
It knows *nothing of the sunrise*
It knows *the dreams I have heard*

Of a sky growing older
Never showing signs of age

I beg the moon for a
Sunset forever
To unblock the drain
To send in a violent rage
The night that swirls down
Everything and myself
This world, my house
The entire neighborhood
The moon and this town

At 2 a.m., wolves overtake her yard

I was in the middle of becoming unlost
When I ended up in the center of a cul-de-sac
On the outskirts of a place they call suburbia
A place where the fog oscillates
Like waves between the maples
Where rows of ferns
Line the fences harboring homes
Where it feels like all that exists
Sits within the cone of a single streetlight

It was then I saw a pack of wolves
Stalking from out of the dark
Into the light of that one streetlight
The four of them marching
With me following close behind
Marching to the house with blue shutters

Once there they tried the front door
Two of them tried to enter through the windows
One by one the wolves
Checked every orifice of that home
But it was clear
They were not getting in

It was then I couldn't believe my mind
As if it had broke
When I saw

One wolf dragging a ladder
By its jaw
And another stood and spoke

"GO AROUND TO THE BACK OF THE HOUSE"
"WE'LL BREAK EVERY WALL"
"WE'LL DESTROY ALL THE GLASS"
"WE'LL CLIMB DOWN THE CHIMNEY"
"SHE WILL NEVER LEAVE"

I was confused, intrigued
I got on all fours, clambering
Into the neighboring yard
Where I climbed
Up a maple tree to see
The backyard of the house
With blue shutters
Where a dozen more wolves
Roamed the lawn
Like sharks
Marched the perimeter
Restless
Their noses angled up
All attention guided to
The second-story window
Which was when I saw
A woman in a sleeping hat
Leaning out halfway
In her hand, she was waving
A bouquet of red meat
With the air of a priestess
Waving a censer
Intoxicating

The wolves stood up their ladder
Rung by rung they climbed
Their eyes in hypnosis spirals
Drawn to the meat
They floated to its smell
Lifted by the chorus of howls below

I shimmied along a branch
To get a better view of the yard
When it snapped and I fell
The wolves surged upon me

I couldn't believe my eyes
It was like my brain had snapped again
Broken like a handful of sticks
Because I saw the wolves were carrying guns
And one was pointed at me
A pistol in my mouth
The wolf said
"PLANT A SIGN IN FRONT OF THE HOUSE"
Which read

"DON'T BOTHER US"
"THERE IS NO ONE HERE"
"WHO NEEDS TO BE SAVED"

More wolves climbed the ladder
Entering through the second-story window
But my accident proved a diversion
The woman was gone
The wolves in her house
Found

The walls were covered in meat
Every nook and cranny
They searched
But they couldn't see a thing
Their eyes were hypnotized
Blind

These wolves were red with rage
They pointed barrels of guns at my face
They forced me
To climb the ladder
Into the meat house
They told me
I'll be their bait
That I'll call out her name
To bring her out
For sacrifice

I asked, Who Am I
With what honors?

Two wolves followed close behind
We walked the hallways lined with meat
Calling out a name I did not know
To no response
Slowly we crept down the stairs
Into her meat kitchen
Where we discovered
We are the sacrifice

The smell of burning wood invaded my nose
I looked out the window and saw
A woman in a sleeping hat

In her sleeping robes
Running away
And to this very day
I believe I heard
The way she was laughing
As if everything had gone to plan
The meat was rotting
The doors were locked
The curtains shut and
The furniture gone

And
Our lungs were full of smoke
A sign out front said

"NO ONE HERE"
"IS TO BE SAVED"

What I hear sleeping in the back of pickup trucks somewhere outside of Manhattan, Kansas

The midnight hour passes over the countryside as if riding on the wind. A chill tickles my skin. I shiver, pull my burlap blanket to my chin, and squeeze it tight. I'm lying on my back in the bed of a pickup truck while the stars flash and twinkle above me. Crickets and bullfrogs chitter, leaves rustle high in the sycamore trees. The air smells like trash, like rubber tires rubbed in acid, or strawberries decomposing into liquid. I'm sick.

I have no idea where I am or how I got here.

I've come to terms with the idea that I'm wasting my life away.

Before, I was filled with such hope.

Around half past midnight, as I'm floating across the ravine between consciousness and sleep, two sets of footsteps approach, crunching in the gravel. Two people. Coming straight to the truck. I'm awake and pull the burlap blanket over my head.

Neither speaks. I can only hear the *crunch crunch crunch* of their steps. The truck's metal doors, driver and passenger side, creak open and then slam shut. Still no talking. The truck doesn't start. I peek out of the sack and see the stars twinkling, and for a second I fear the whole thing is a figment of my imagination. Maybe I was asleep. The truck engine roars to life, and the whole metallic chassis quivers as if ejaculating. As it jerks down the road, stopping and starting, the two in the vehicle start to speak; they are arguing. I listen:

Of all the ways you show me
You love me
You pretend to live in my head

The other says:

Sure, and you?
Looking my way with
Eyes of disgust.
You who amble across the floor.

First:

I have never seen disgust
My eyes only amble to you
But then you pull the drapes shut
And—voilà—disappear

Drapes!
Why, your heart is no better.
You can't say a word!

I've been nothing but kind
And clear

Hah. Clear like a witch.
Hag of the graveyard shift.

Stop the car stop the car now stop it

The truck screeches to a halt. The momentum drives my head into the metal body of the cab. I nearly cry "ouch," but I clasp my hands over my mouth just in time, as I'm positive they would've heard. I touch my scalp expecting blood, but I find none, although a lump is already forming.

One of the truck doors creaks open, and only one set of shoes crunches on the pavement. Unlike the slow rhythm before, this time one of them is running. *Pap pap pap pap* goes the crunching gravel.

"Wait!" the driver says, "I'll put the radio on! I'm sorry!"

But the words float up in the air, into the stratosphere to melt with the stars and space, and they fall on no ears but God's and my own.

The passenger is gone; the driver walks in a circle, giving me a soothing rhythm of gravel crunches. There are two times when the driver punches the side of the truck. I close my eyes and pretend to be invisible. I hear a "fuck fuck fuck." I hear the passenger's name. "Fuck fuck fucking fuck." I hear the door slam, the truck roaring to life. Above me, God is holding the stars still. We are moving. Streetlights pass one by one. *Flash! one two three four; flash! one two three four.* The driver turns a corner and slows to a steady pace.

"Come back!" The driver calls out into the night. "Come back to me!"

The car slows to a stop.

"Hey."
Hey

Doors slam. The metal truck quivers and roars to life and picks up speed. The streetlights move faster. *Flash! One-two. Flash! One-two.*

Where did you go
I could hear your pleas

I was cold.

Later, and I swear it must be nearing morning, the truck is as silent and unmoving as the night. We're parked outside of a small, rusty, beige-colored clapboard home. I pull the blanket to my chin. The sky is now black, and there are no more stars. A few scattered dark clouds are thin and transparent and barely visible. I think: God watches every one of us. It's not a deep thought. It's more a remembrance of the greatest terror I have ever known.

I'm soon to be dreaming, which will be watched by God, and I feel a pain in my chest over the bare minimum I've done in this life. I'm wondering how I came to be in the back of a pickup truck. It's so quiet that, from the house, I think I hear one of them say:

"The bed is warm."

The words float up toward the stratosphere, and the light in the house goes dark.

The next morning, after I bathe in a creek and wash the dirt out of my wrinkles, and after I clean my crusted hair, I take a seat in a red leather booth at the roadside diner out on Highway 18. A clock made of car rims hangs on the wall above my booth, ticking slowly. A woman in her sixties I've never met takes my order—pancakes, and coffee—and the words I hear are:

"Stop fucking worrying, you cunt. We're all just waiting to die."

These words make me content
They alleviate my fears
But maybe I misunderstood
And so I dine

Hallucinating a corpse town behind a storm cloud

The train master checks his pocket watch
"All aboard!" he says as
Steam billows from beneath the train
The steel clinks, scrapes, and whistles
"No!" I say
I will not leave
I shake my head and tuck my knees
"I refuse to come aboard."
He looks me up and down
With a disgusted sneer
"Fine. Why would I care
What you do?
What you say?
I can't wait all day."
The offense I feel
It burns

I march away
I stomp my duck feet
Down the station steps
Waddle-crossing the street
To a bakery
The furious smell of coffee
Teeth tear into a donut
Jelly

There my eyes become a blue-black-blue
From a lack of sleep for days
Waited waited waited awake

After I continue
I march and I stomp
Duck feet half asleep
Across a bridge
To a neighborhood
Where the doors slam shut
Windows boarded closed
When a thing like me
Goes
Where a woman
Calls
For her mother
She is saying

"All aboard!"

I say, for the thousandth fucking time
"No!"
I will not go
But there is nothing I can do
I'm trapped and old
I turn around and
What do I see
I'm at the station again
Where the train master smiles
And checks his pocket watch
As steam billows from beneath the train
"I promise we'll get you there."
Safe
I tell him to look at the rusted tracks
Weathered and brittle iron cast
I say I'll die if I take your train
So again, duck feet, I waddle away

This time I head in another direction
I march to the top of a hill
To the summit I look back down
Through a hole in the clouds
A town that glistens to the sound
Of tracks that leave the station
They bend
They break
And I go
I'm back at the station
The train master looks at his pocket watch
"All aboard!"
I take my seat
I try to remember
I will not go

Letter from the Trash #3

Surabaya, Indonesia. A stone's throw south of the equator. When winter comes to the city, the three million people living there move as the earth turns, and a warm wetness falls from an icy sky.

I was visiting Surabaya during monsoon season, and I felt an icy wind in my spine as droplets of sweat slid down my back. I was not cold; I was not warm; I was soaked from my jacket to the marrow in my bones. And I was confused. Each raindrop was a sliver digging beneath my skin.

It was night, and the darkness was thick, like air you waded through, and I stood on what looked like the lightless corner of a busy intersection where the airport bus had dropped me off only moments before.

"Your stop!" The bus driver yelled three times before catching my attention. "Hey! This is your stop!"

His English was immaculate; his memory was shit. This was not my stop. But I panicked and obeyed without checking the map on my phone. Only after the bus zoomed away did I discover I was miles from the hostel where I had reserved a warm, cozy bed that I had romanticized about all afternoon. Now it was just a mirage, somewhere out there. Somewhere dry.

I was in a city I didn't know. A country I didn't know. The language was a mystery.

I asked myself, Why did I come to this country? Why did I run away?

I did not run away.

I was thousands of miles away, standing on the corner watching the endless flow of motorbikes materializing out of the darkness like fish swept in a river's current, engines purring as they got closer from one direction, only to disappear into another darkness in the other direction, a darker darkness where no light could enter.

Row after row of motorbikes appeared and disappeared. The smell of oil leapt from the pavement, mixing with rain and runoff from tropical palms. An oversized camion passed by like a giant log floating on this black river of motorbike fish. A motorbike slowed in front of me, and a man wearing a helmet with a face shield and an oversized rain poncho said something in Indonesian. I shook my head. "No no no, sorry sorry."

He shrugged and drove off.

He seemed normal. He was likely asking if I needed a ride, but, not knowing the language, I hadn't a clue. These are the things I feel in my gut, but I have no proof.

I was a woman alone in a foreign land.

I was completely unprepared and unable to defend myself. Still am.

This experience in Surabaya was just one example.

I was the cliché American in a foreign land who is raped and killed and burned and buried all alone, in a rice field where nobody will ever find my bones.

This, too, felt true.

Another motorbike stopped. The driver wasn't wearing a helmet or a poncho and was dripping on the pavement. His hair was flat against his head, and he had kind eyes. He looked like someone who had been wet for a long time. I said, in English, "No no no" and waved him away.

Alone.

Killed. Raped. Burned alive.

I didn't know how I would get to the hostel.

Right at that moment, the rain stopped, and I concluded that I would walk.

And that's when the third bike pulled up. Two men on a motorbike, with square faces and loose, bright-colored clothing, pulled up alongside me. One had a tooth protruding from his tightly pinched lips. The other was cross-eyed and wore a hat with octopus arms. They were dry, young, and scrawny, which meant if they tried anything nefarious, it was me who could do the raping, killing, and burning. It was a twisted thought.

Where are you going? They asked in English.

I said, *I'm going to my hostel.*

They pointed at me and asked if I was sick. They said I looked pale and frozen. That I was the whitest white person they'd ever seen. Do I need a ride? I do.

Would you like a ride?

I laughed. I stood on the precipice of an unknown: a safe, warm shower at the hostel was minutes away.

I nodded.

Was I being unreasonable? Smart? Stupid?

Is this how the American gets taken? Scrawny nerdy teens?

Reluctantly, I climbed on their motorbike, taking a place between the two. The seat was barely large enough for the two of them, and with me as the third passenger, the one with the octopus hat in the rear balanced on the very back of the triangle-shaped seat; as the motorbike took off, he was only able to hold on by wrapping his arms around the driver in front, making me the centerpiece of an Indonesian sandwich. There was now no turning back. The wind made my drying arms shiver.

The driver in front was asking questions. *Where are you from? Why are you here in Indonesia? Are you married? Why are you alone?*

I answered each with short, polite phrases. *Where did you learn English? You speak really well*, I said.

We all speak English here, the octopus hat man said.

More or less, the toothy one in front said.

The motorbike weaved in and out of traffic, gliding through the river of bikes and the whale-like camions. The air had a sweet scent to it from the fried rice stands they passed.

Fear had almost completely left me when the motorbike came to a stop.

Your hostel, the octopus hat man in the back said. He tapped my shoulders and pointed to the right. *Yes? Your hostel?*

I unstuck myself from between the two. The one in back plopped my luggage on the ground next to me, and he gave me the largest grin I had ever seen. I turned to the hostel entrance and looked down the thin walkway between white concrete buildings. Rows of white-lit umbrellas stuck in the ground loomed over plastic patio tables. Spiky ferns sat quietly on both sides of a concrete walkway. A little sign said "Bonnet Hostel—Cheap". I could feel the warm shower within.

How long will you be in Surabaya, the driver said.

We'd be happy to show you around.

Yes, what are you doing tomorrow?

Meet tomorrow for coffee? I know the best place for coffee.

I said, *I'm sorry but I can't,* and thanked them. I pulled out my wallet. The driver was offended, and the two left.

I walked into the hostel.

Safe.

Signed: Surabaya, August 2022

A new place

The midnight train races
Through the early morning hours
As if it didn't have any brakes
Spiraling out of control
Rocking back and forth like waves
Like walking a tightrope on tracks
Over a bridge, over water
We teeter
Over a watery grave
A river that rushes out to the sea
Leaving the world behind we knew
Behind its long arid flats

I guess the train knows where to go
As if it had a mind of its own
But the mind of a train is dead: lights flicker
Barreling like Frankenstein's monster
Rotted wood in the walls swells
I smell
Rusted cast iron
And wonder if I'll make it home

Because I know I won't
I will live above the station
At the top of Marigold Hill

Where I have no one to ask
If this is the right place
If the train rocks back and forth
If it drifts me to sleep
I'm dreaming of my bed, my desk
A TV and a chair
It's all I ask for

But when I wake
It's because the gold-trimmed gables
Are cracking from the salty air

The midnight train plunges into the sea
A new place it was not destined to be
Six long cars rusted and abandoned
Swallowed by the water
No one else falls with me
Except for the conductor and me
We've been left to die

By the time I arrive
The marigolds are dry
And this autumn night freezes
To me
Forever at the brink of winter
Watched by the faces of my home

The faces blemished and poisoned
The faces with an urge to leave
I see them at the station
Waiting

The midnight train snakes alongside a river
Slithering away, undisturbed
Cutting through an overgrown forest
Claustrophobic
The trees constrict
Tighter and tighter
Cutting off our oxygen
The train swims deeper into the water

I am certain this train knows where to find
My home
But the train's mind is dead: the light flickers
And my new house is above the station
In Marigold Hills
But the marigolds are dry
Dead
A corpse town flows on a raft
Downstream
Carried by the floodwater
And a memory
I once had
Of the rains that used to be

The midnight train follows a river
Through the early morning hours
Which rushes out to sea

I HEAR LIGHT LOUD AT 3 A.M.

I took a stone to the gut
The day I knew
I would not be easy to fool again
But I'm not so hard to kill
Still, I came to you stumbling
Off on another trip again
The wind has left me
It never came easy
To be the one who goes
To be the one to turn sour
Because it occurred to me
One day in the future I'll look back
At all this time
I spent gazing straight at the bottom
A clean line of sight
To where the streetlight meets the sky
Hints of an acrid morning
This neighborhood soul awakens
With neon green pollution as the only light

It was not like the time you stopped by
Your silence made me feel like a kid again
Even though we didn't go
To the playground
We're polluted
Extended
Like all the pretty houses dotting the valley

We're touched by rain in misty little drops
We've sheltered in place

Until the storm in this valley went under
The water cold and violent
Rushed to the house at the end of the road
Broke through every window. I spied
The shimmers of our street below
You saw me gasp as I tried to swim
You saw me take off on a run

Because I could hear the light louder then
At 3 a.m.

Because it was after the darkness but before
Lightness
Opposite gloaming
We're polluted
Reversed like twilight
Became light like liquid
Poured over
The tops of the rocky hills around us

There was no going back
I fell headfirst into the storm
From the life I knew
No fear of a bottom
Or morning
To find
Anything
Far away
What the future holds
What came before

My 4 a.m. park friend, Michelle

It's now 4 a.m. and
I'm wide awake and
I have eyes like
Electricity
I'm shocked by the desire to see
But unsure of what to do
About it so I go
To the far end of the park
Where I know
I'll find an old friend
Michelle with the gray smile
Thin and dainty as ever
A look just like a vampire
Proud as ever
To be sitting
On a brand-new park bench

In her hands she holds
A half loaf of bread
Which she tears into
Inch-by-inch cubes that she
Stores in a frayed cotton pouch
For the crows, she says as I approach
As I shiver from the cold
The dead stare
"It's gonna be a brutal October night and

Tomorrow it will be a
Skyless
November day."

"Skyless is beautiful as you know."

I tell her I know better than most
and take out
Prosciutto and bread and cheese for
The night sandwich I prepare for
Us
On these nights
I take what remains
Of her half-loaf
I ask her if she heard
About this new thing the papers call "SPIR"
She says, "No, but can I have a little bread
To save for when I feed the birds?"

I shake my head
"Have you eaten tonight, Michelle?"

Slather on the mayonnaise
Layer the lettuce like
Tucking in a child
Sending them to sleep

I tell her I first heard of SPIR
On the train yesterday
A voice came over the P.A.
Crackled, distorted
A glitch
A woman said

"Tomorrow *SPIR SPIR SPIR*
on a cloudy winter day."

I lean over and tell Michelle
—"It was a lie. It was skyless like I was and
We were, and still are, in the grip of autumn's trauma."

Michelle laughs
"Perhaps this winter will *SPIR*."
SPIR FUCKING SPIR
She inspects the sandwich I made for her
Every pickle in its right place
Prosciutto perfectly placed
She wipes tears from her eyes and
Claims my mind must be broken
As holy as the cheese

I say, "Holy like your shoes?"

Of course, she says
"Madness is close to obvious.
As holiness is godliness."
She's silent for a minute
She nibbles at the bread
With the tip of her front teeth
Like a squirrel
"I'm thinking about this SPIR and
What it could mean."

"It's not obvious at all,"
I say
"Even in this park with its
Soft padded walls."

With a sandwich in one hand
Her frayed cotton pouch in the other
My friend Michelle and I
Wait for the birds and their canvas tents
To arrive and
Live
In dusty patches of dirt
Swarming with bees and memories

Together we feed
We offer food and
Wait
Confident the sun will rise
The birds will rise
To this day I remember she said
"This SPIR, I'll never understand,
Why we insist we're great?
Because we're only here to feed the birds."

The ghosts of this town

I hate to be the one to tell you
About the ghosts right here in this town
Billions that float all around you
Surrounding you
And where I am now
Watch: I can move through them
As if I'm swimming through water
I can push them aside
Like curtains
I breathe them in
And exhale
The ghosts float out of my ears
They hang by the tip of my nose
So come, swim with me
Through this sea of ghosts
Through the rooms of the dead
The streets of the dead
This town of the dead
But I must remind you
As you swim from one place to the next
And go wherever it is you go
Wherever you feel like
You'll be you and
The ghosts will be taking
—Notes

Their book about me has volumes
The size of an encyclopedia
Every word written by ghosts
Under the cover of night
They read to me
This book they wrote about me
And until the sun comes back
They'll laugh at me

Because they see me as a fool
And they see you too
They see I fake at living
They know my days are hollow
I let time slip through my fingers because
I have thousands, tens of thousands, times left
The sun sleeps by the window

And that's me
But the ghosts around you
Are judging you too

Your ghosts and mine
The ghosts of this town
Archivists of time
One day there'll simply be too many
The ground will be stuffed with corpses
The ghosts will combine
They'll come to your house and break all your lights
They'll send us all into one last fever dream

Listen now and with care
And you can hear them promise
Terrible things

Like how in death you feel at home
How you don't have to pass in the dark
With no one around
To care for you
Who, with words so quiet
Hardly speak
But listen and with care and you hear
About how a life well lived
Goes on forever

Which makes me wonder about me—my ghost
The one I'll eventually leave here in this town
I wonder about the size of it
Will I be as white as a bedsheet?
Or as transparent as glass?
I wonder about the way I'll go, "Boo!"
Or what's the role of my sadness in this
Or how I can't leave my ghost anywhere I like
Or how I can't leave many ghosts
Peppered around the globe
Planted like seeds in the field
As numerous as mountaintops
As weightless as bubbles floating across the Atlantic

One day, and I can't say when
I'll join this squadron of ghosts
And then, later, your ghosts
And mine
Will combine
And go to your house and break your lights
And send us our last fever dream
Only then do they end
With one more note
One that lets them laugh

Waiting for the sun to get its comeuppance

At 6 am, it's official: I've been awake all night
There's a skittishness in my veins
My arms are like octopus arms
My soul is a trash can overflowing
Because my body won't go
To sleep
I know it's irrational
For one who's been awake too long
The fear I'll explode
This body, viscous flesh bomb
Bursting in all directions
With liquid meat splashed against the wall
This is what I mean when I say
An orchestra of guts
Drips down the wallpaper
There are bones in the tile
From the ceiling
Blood showers down
If I listen, I hear
The screams of those who love me
They wake up half the town
Because it's always an ungodly hour
I close my eyes and wait
Lids like razor blades
At 6 a.m., my head is a gutter
And I drink all this junk from the street
Until I've imagined the way you dress

The way you slide into underwear
My head is in a dumpster
And yours is a hand that waves away the fever
A disembodied liver working as a telepath
That gives the gift of sleep to strangers
That sends signals to my heart and tells it to beat faster
All this—at 6 a.m.
When the baby birds call me master
For I am a worm
Devoured, I say wait
Look
The morning light rolls in like a fog
You can see it painted on the hilltops
Just then
The wooden doors of my bedroom creak open
They let the morning light in
And wooden halls echo
Sizzling bacon from the kitchen
Toilets flush and showers run
My hope flickers like a candle
My breath like a sewer
I see your shadow
You're dressed in an apron
Like silence pressed on my neck
Like the heel of a boot
Until I hear the electricity in the walls
Outside in the distance
A thunderstorm dawdles
The porch light is off
You fly around my room
Burned as white as the morning
You may see me here, deprived
Shadows that pull me out of bed

As if I were a marionette
And you were on a stage
And just like that
I'm standing up and
You disappear
And then I hear nothing with my disembodied ear
Because at this hour I'm a glob
My thoughts are like nails tapping on the glass
My thoughts are like the sound of breaking glass
And I recognize your turgor
Your skin, your real-life finger!
My skittish blood spills like a cup filled beyond the brim
And I am a landfill
A flying worm sack tossed into
The feeding lands of birds
The power lines, burnt, cooked
Frying the sky until it releases a blue light ash
The birds sing like pigs on the way to slaughter
My alarm clock like a drill burrowing laughter
I'm awake
For a moment in time, I see you
Watching me from the foot of our bed
As golden morning light peeks in
I reach out to touch your hand and I'm not sure what I grab
And I explode
Again and again and again

A Holistic Melody for a Good Time

If you're lonely I can give you

A smoke-stack industrial zone
With rising plumes of ash
Decrepit factories made of brick
Steel viaducts rusted brown

If you're lonely you can clap
Give yourself a high five

You can take a hand
With your other hand
And go for a stroll
Across town, nowhere to go
Together

The jazz band packs up for the night

In the old, rusty part of town
The wooden fences are painted
In a way that reminds me of November
Cold and electrified, cozy inside
Here the streets are wide and the walls buckle
From dark windows come red eyes sparkling
Amidst the wails of the ghost musicians
Who play until the light comes up
At the start of a new day
And the ghosts rise up
Strumming a low E
Tuning their strings
They blow the spit out of the brass
And you hear a sound
A coarse growl rising
Deep underneath your feet
In the old, rusty part of town

There, the softest light glows from within the corner bars
Dreams of ghosts fall from the stars
They are sifted into the ether
They spill and sometimes they flood
The streets
And it's like they'll be washed down the gutter

I raise my arms
My toes grow roots
I have decided
I will become a tree
In the old, rusty part of town

There the jazz bands pack up their gear for the night
The music scratches their ears like nettles
They pack into a van and tonight
They will leave our town and brave the valley
Riding in silence past the pockets of groves
On the very edge of the forest
Practicing their finale
The morning is upon them
An orchestra of sound
The next show for when the sun goes down
A dinner of cigarettes and red wine

In the old, rusty part of town

Where the birds sing Mozart
And the air tastes like oil

In the old, rusty part of town
As I walk through every lawn
For at this hour, the bakeries wake
On the corner, a man washes the sidewalk
In front of his shop
He waves at a woman, led by dogs, who walks
With footsteps shuffled, muffled
A bus pulls up to the curb and stops
And the morning light snaps the horizon

I raise my arms
I walk the sidewalk off Main
Past the school, past the cafe
Past the firehouse, past the library
And I'm reminded: there are no emperors here
The ghosts are tethered to their dreams

In the old, rusty part of town
Woodland king

The dead hold their memories dear
And their shadows stretch like taffy
They cut the dawn, they refract light
It means I've made it through the night
And now I'm here: morning

A morning unlike any other morning

The time has come for me to go.
The night has come to an end.
I have no car, I have no money.
I'm pulled away from here.

I see the sun has risen,
The cold night has broken.
From sleep, I'm culled like a thread,
To hang and dry beneath a bright blue sky.

I hear alarms like digital bells,
From the houses I pass
On my walk out of town.
Until cornfields appear.

I turn to wave and say goodbye,
Although no one will remember me.
My excitement burns like fear,
As a hand pulls me away from here.

Today is a new day.
Yesterday meant very little after all.
When I enter the corn I am a child reborn,
Yet I think, I am one of the same.

Because one day,
A morning unlike any other morning,
We will see
This new adventure
We've become.

Letter from the Trash #4

A man on drugs sprints toward me with his longboard raised high above his head. He is unshaven, his hair a mess of bedhead and crunchy grit like dried semen. His skin—dried and cracked from life on the Denver streets, baked by the desert sun at a mile high—looks like beef jerky. The air here steals moisture like a debt.

The man reminds me of how America was cursed by the natives who were hunted by the white settlers; the phrase "The only good Indian is a dead Indian" makes the place more cursed than others. The crazed look in his eyes speaks of his intention to bring that board hard down upon my head. Everyone who lives here is hunted, diseased, disgraced. Ultimately erased. The junkie channels the pain of the past to become superhuman. He channels the miners and riders and the army that killed the natives in the mountains. He channels the Utes, the Navajo, the Sioux.

The Denver sun beats down; the man runs toward me.

My little dog, an ancient cocker spaniel who shakes, is nestled in my arms. It is seven in the morning on a Saturday, and there are no people in American downtowns. Because of course it is. There are no people in Denver. In America. Why would there be? Saturday summer sunrise hits like a waterfall.

A man on drugs raises his longboard over his head. "Stop! Stop! Stop! Stop!" he yells, and I have no idea what he means.

I was crossing the street while the "Do Not Walk" hand was a solid red. It's the only thing I can think of stopping; it is the only thing I think of that might be *stopped*.

My wife falls to the ground. I step between him and my family, I hold my dog tighter, and I am ready to run. The man on drugs is a thousand feet high, and I'm small in his shadow.

Something changes. He changes. The man on drugs changes direction. He turns to the left and something new and shiny, worthy of his skateboard, his rage, catches his eye. I look to see what has captured his attention, to see what stopped him from killing me.

It is a red Toyota RAV4. Beautifully glistening in the Denver Saturday morning sunlight. His skateboard still raised, the man approaches the RAV4. The RAV4 does nothing in return. It does not fall to the ground; it is not shocked. It does not curse these lands. And so the man on drugs brings the skateboard through the back window. One, two, three to-the-bleacher swings. And off he runs. This is what happens. The sun comes back.

Signed: Denver, August 2022

Epilogue

I no longer wander alone
Joy and suffering are once again in equilibrium
There is balance here

I feel as if my experiences in this town, this region, are akin to
a dirty white shirt being thrown into a washing machine with extra
bleach. The chemicals have made me clean again. But too many
chemicals, especially the strong ones, for too long of time, will ruin
me. They ruin everything.

I am free from the curse I mentioned all those pages ago
I am free of that witch who visited me randomly on a random
night
I am free of my memories and my tragedies

And only one question remains
For me and for you
You who will close this book shortly

What should we do next?

And for this, there is only one answer

We go on an adventure
Wander together
Of course